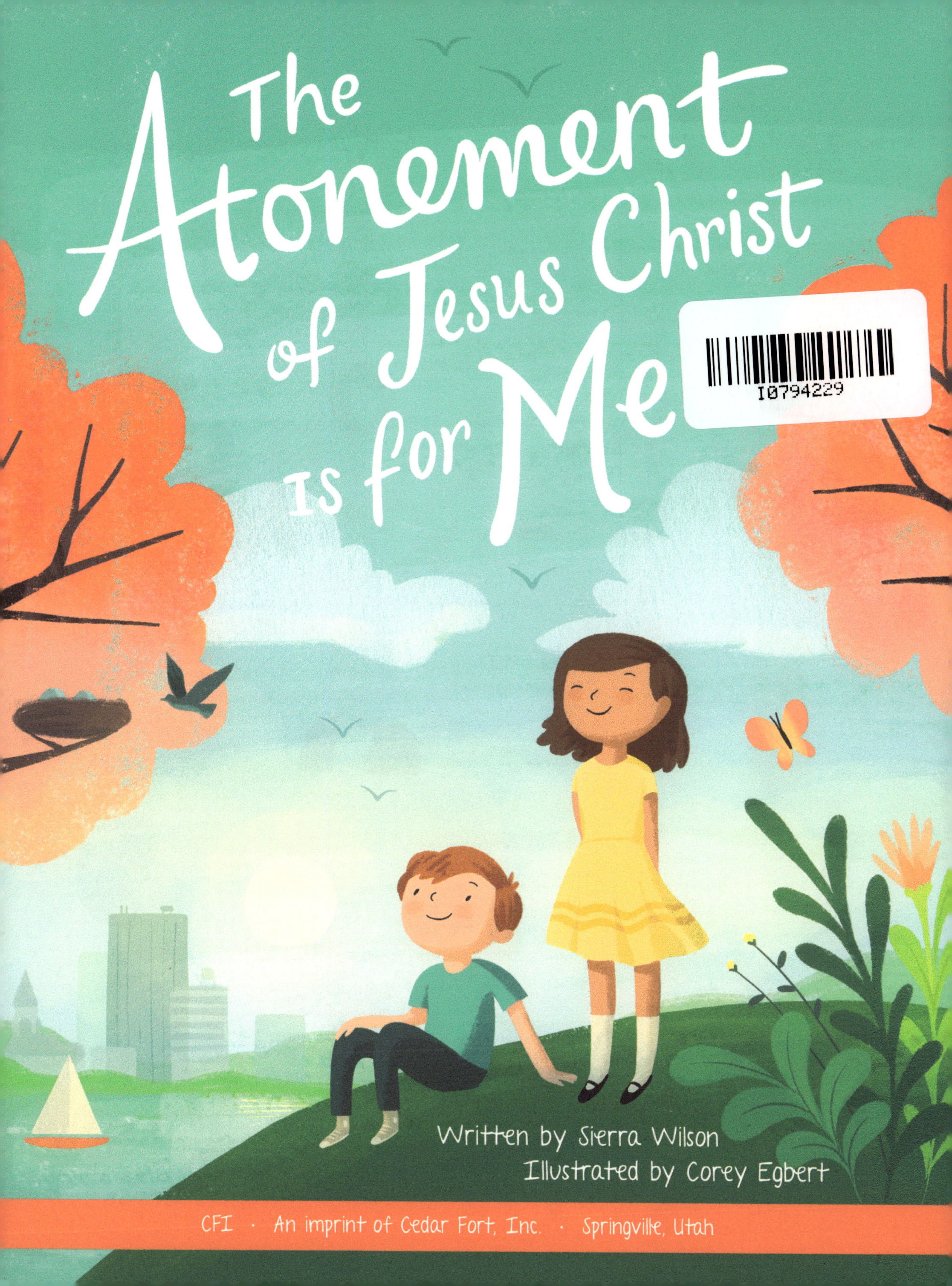
The Atonement of Jesus Christ Is for Me
Written by Sierra Wilson
Illustrated by Corey Egbert
CFI · An imprint of Cedar Fort, Inc. · Springville, Utah
I0794229

What is the Atonement?
What is that word?

It's the greatest gift
in all the world!

Jesus Christ came to earth
because He loves us so much.

His Atonement blesses everyone
with His special touch.

Jesus gave His life
for you and for me
so we can repent
and be happy and free.

And because Jesus died for us
and now lives again,

we'll live again too,
with our family and friends.

To use His Atonement,
you just need to pray.

Ask Jesus to help you
each night and each day.

When we make a bad choice
or do something wrong,

Jesus can help us
to change and be strong.

We can say sorry,
be honest and true.

We can do things
that are so hard to do.

When we feel scared,
or lonely, or sad,

Jesus can help us
feel peaceful and glad.

But what if I'm having a really hard day?

Jesus will love you
and show you the way.

His Atonement is gentle
like a kiss on your cheek.

His Atonement is
quiet like a little
mouse squeak.

And what if I'm hurting
down deep in my heart?

Jesus understands you and knows where to start.

His Atonement is stronger
than storms on the sea.

His Atonement goes higher than the tallest oak tree.

With Jesus's help,
we can all do good deeds.

We can cheer up a friend
or help someone in need.

Jesus knows how to help you become the best you.

He wants to guide you
all your life through.

What is the Atonement?
Is it for me?
Yes, it's Christ's gift
that He gives lovingly.

For my sweetheart, Chris,
who always cheered me on and for
all the children in my life who inspire me
—Sierra

For Oliver
—Corey

ISBN 13: 978-1-4621-4073-2

Published by CFI, an imprint of Cedar Fort, Inc.
2373 W. 700 S., Springville, UT 84663
Distributed by Cedar Fort, Inc., www.cedarfort.com

Library of Congress Control Number: 2018936989

Cover design and typesetting by Shawnda T. Craig
Cover design © 2018 Cedar Fort, Inc.
Edited by Kaitlin Barwick

Printed in the United States of America

10 9 8 7 6 5 4 3 2 1

Printed on acid-free paper